MIKE'S UNFORGETTABLE ST. LOUIS HISTORY FOR KIDS

written by Mike Kleckner

illustrated by Erin Hopkins

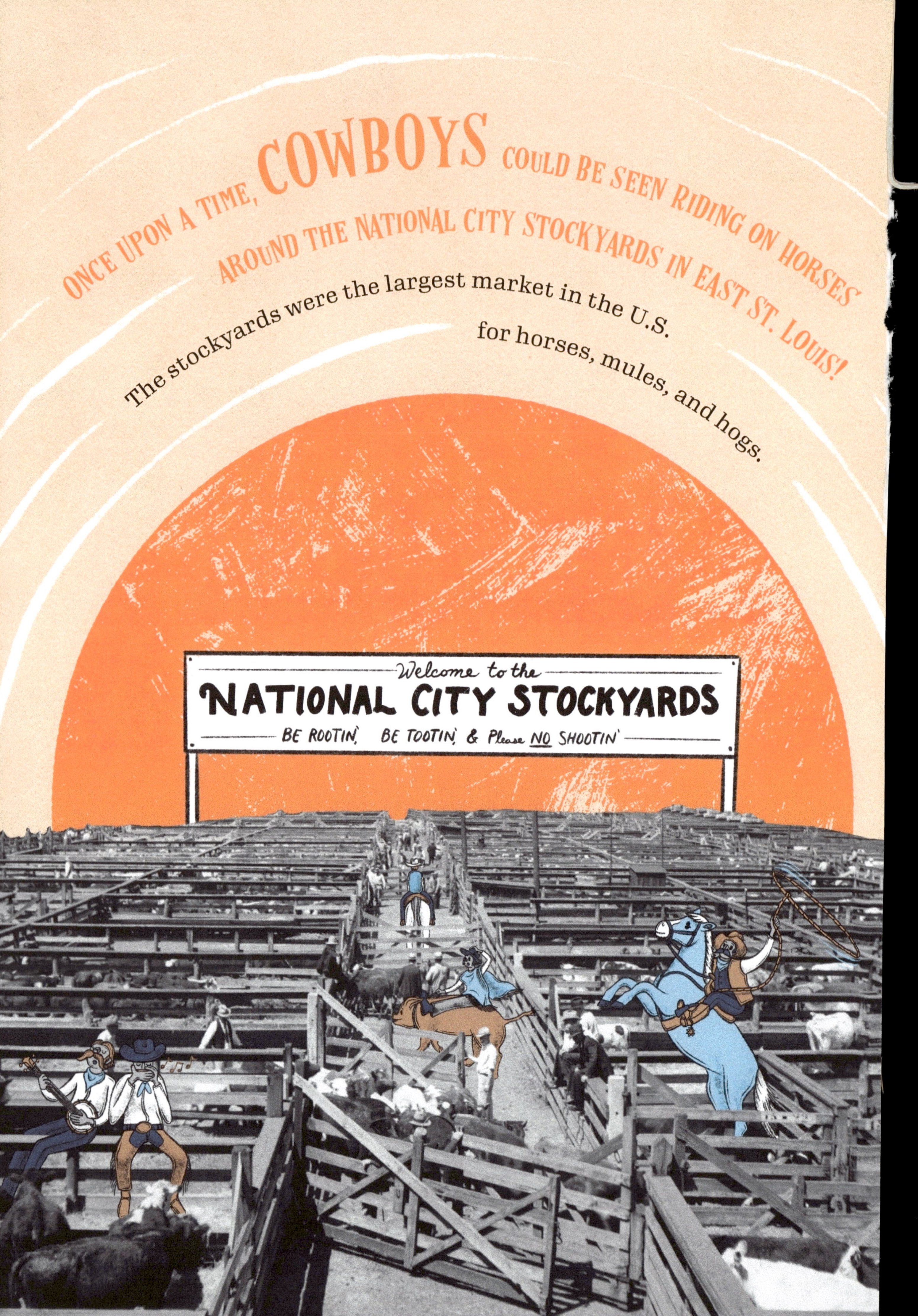

ONCE UPON A TIME, COWBOYS COULD BE SEEN RIDING ON HORSES AROUND THE NATIONAL CITY STOCKYARDS IN EAST ST. LOUIS!
The stockyards were the largest market in the U.S. for horses, mules, and hogs.
Welcome to the
NATIONAL CITY STOCKYARDS
BE ROOTIN', BE TOOTIN', & Please NO SHOOTIN'

THE SAINTE GENEVIEVE ACADEMY

was the first public school west of the Mississippi.

It was built in the early 1800s from the stone blocks of a **FRENCH FORT** that was torn down and carried across the river from Illinois.

Have you ever taken the elevator up to the top of the

GATEWAY ARCH?

The trams in the Arch were built by the St. Louis Car Company, which mostly built **BUSES AND TROLLEYS.**

Did you know that St. Louis is home to one of the first **SKYSCRAPERS** in the U.S.?

The Wainwright Building was the first building to be constructed with a steel frame!

Do you like story time? In 1907, the St. Louis Public Library's
Barr Branch hosted the library system's first story time for children.

Statues of a **LION, TORTOISE,** and **HARE**
greeted children as they entered the library!

CHARLES BOLIN provided the money needed to create Kellogg's Corn Flakes in 1905 with $30,000, which would be worth just under one million dollars today!

Did you know a St. Louis company made the first PLAY DOUGH!? Absorene sold play dough, which was advertised by popular children's entertainers like Walt Disney as a

"PINK BALL OF MAGIC"

long before the Play-Doh company made a similar product in the 1930s.

FRIEDRICH JAHN, the father of gymnastics, founded a gymnastic community in 1811. You can find a statue of Jahn in Forest Park, but it is missing his MUSCULAR ARMS!

There is ALWAYS room in your tummy for chocolate and popcorn, right?

CHOCOLATES, POPCORN, & BUTTERY CARAMELS

were made in St. Louis by the Blanke-Wenneker Candy Company during the early 1900s.

GUS' PRETZEL SHOP
on Arsenal Street has been serving pretzels for over 100 YEARS
and believes its stick shape is unique to St. Louis.

Gus'
PRETZELS

DAVID R. FRANCIS

is the only person to serve as both St. Louis mayor and Missouri governor.

In 1916 on Christmas Eve, Francis donated 60 acres of land that later became FRANCIS PARK in St. Louis Hills.

For an upset tummy, some kids chew on TUMS. TUMS have been made in St. Louis for over 90 years.

And can you believe SweeTARTS were originally created by putting PIXY STIX powder through the machines at the TUMS factory?

So, if your tummy feels icky from eating too many SweeTARTS, eat some TUMS!

St. Louis has nearly **50 CAVES**, more than any other city in the United States. Inside the caves are **STREAMS**, **WATERFALLS**, and the burial grounds of **PREHISTORIC ANIMALS**.

In 1840, a giant skeleton was unveiled at a dime museum on the St. Louis riverfront. A newspaper ad called the beast a

MISSOURI LEVIATHAN

that "made the earth tremble under the step of his feet." A three-piece band was even hired to play

INSIDE ITS RIB CAGE!

This skeleton was really several mastodon skeletons put together!

Have you ever ridden on the St. Louis Carousel at

FAUST PARK?

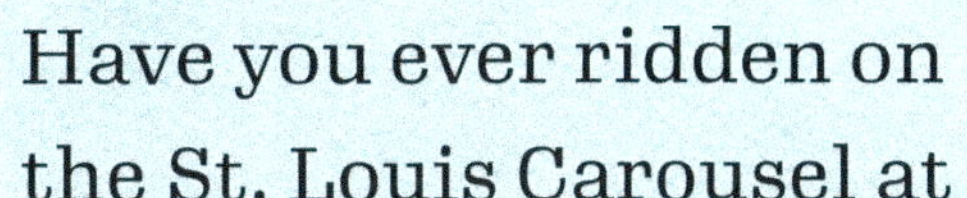

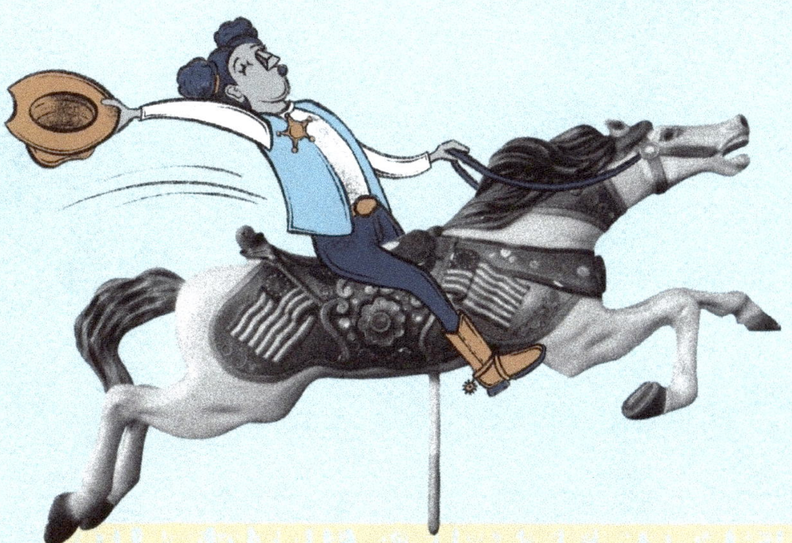

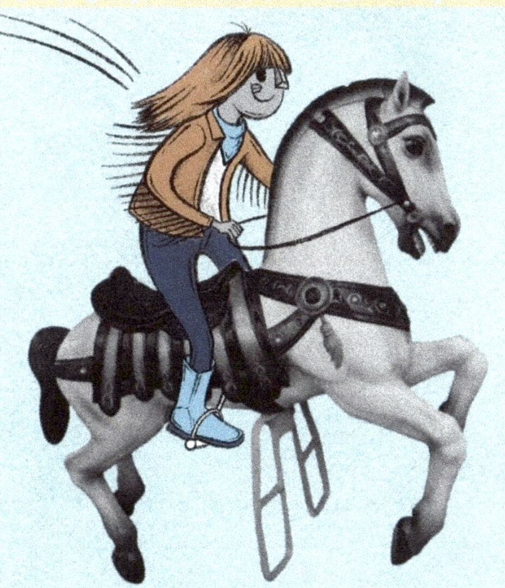

Sixty hand-carved horses, four deer, and two sleighs whirl the happy kids around and around.

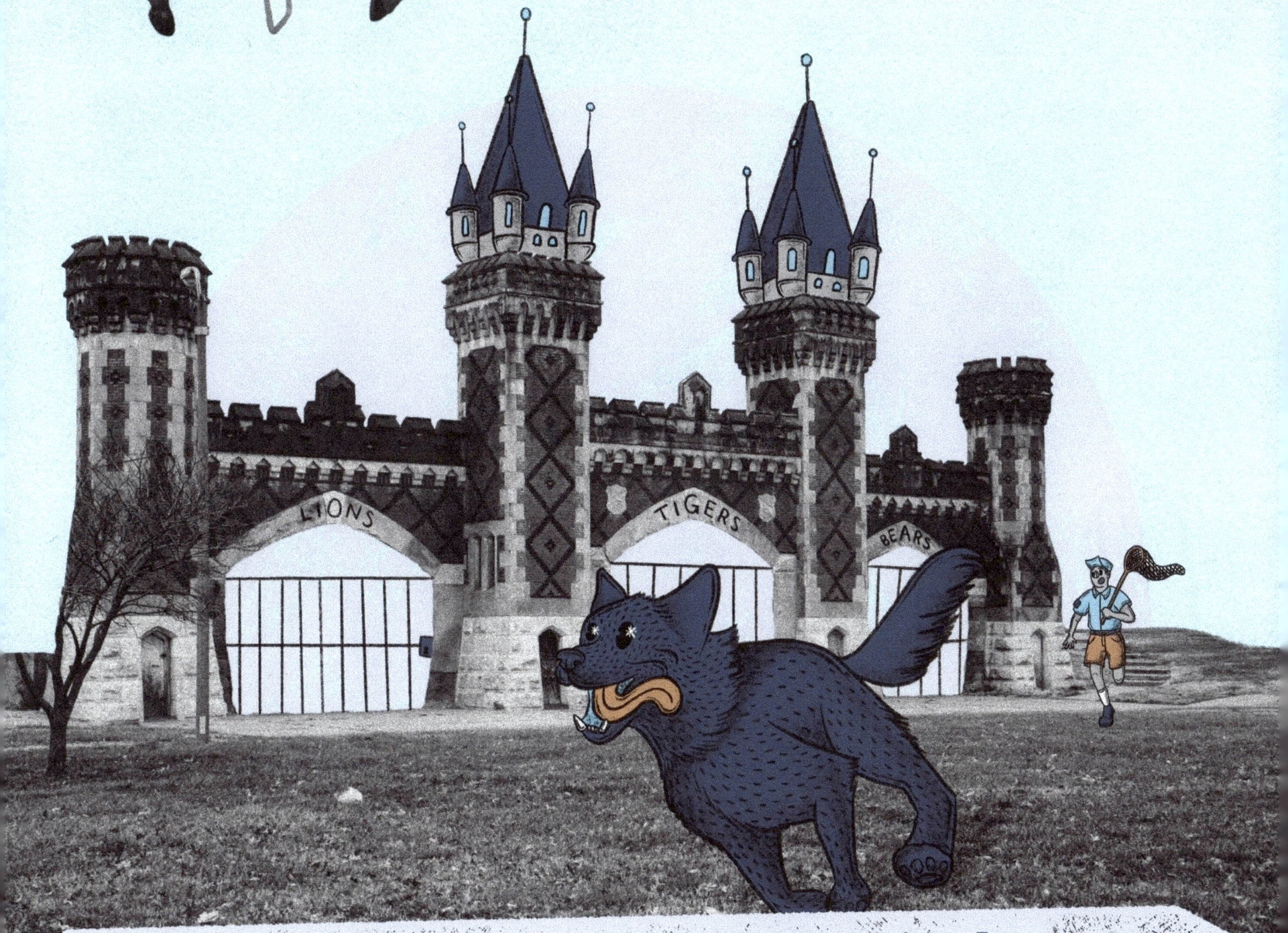

A castle wall from 1876 can be seen at **FAIRGROUND PARK**. It is all that is left from St. Louis's first zoo. The zoo had bear pits, llamas, antelopes, tapirs, kangaroos, and a water hog. One time, a black wolf **ESCAPED** and led the zookeepers on a five-mile chase!

Getting from **DOWNTOWN** to **FOREST PARK** used to take 40 minutes by carriage!

Robert Wadlow, from Alton, IL, was the He was known around the world as the Alton Giant. His furniture, clothing, and car required many changes. One pair of his size 37 shoes would cost about the same as 23 pairs of shoes today.

In 1952,
MENLO SMITH
opened the Fruzola
Company of St. Louis.

FRUZOLA was a
sugary powder
used to make
candies, including
Fun Dip, Pixy
Stix, SweeTARTS,
Sprees, and Nerds.

Fruzola

DELICIOUS-
NESS
TANK No. 4

Have you visited the

FLIGHT CAGE

at the St. Louis Zoo? Did you know it is one of the only remaining structures from the **1904 WORLD'S FAIR!?**

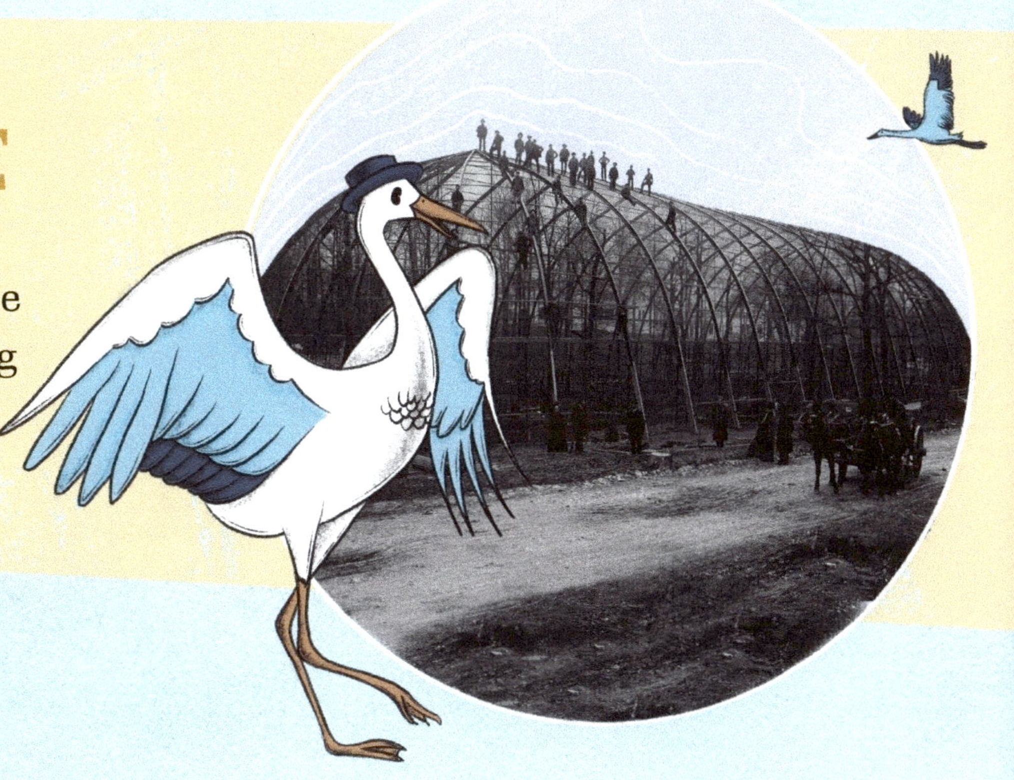

JOHN A. MCARTHUR

founded local sporting goods chain **JOHNNY MAC'S** in an old donut shop. If you played sports around St. Louis before 2019, you likely wore Johnny Mac's uniforms and used their equipment.

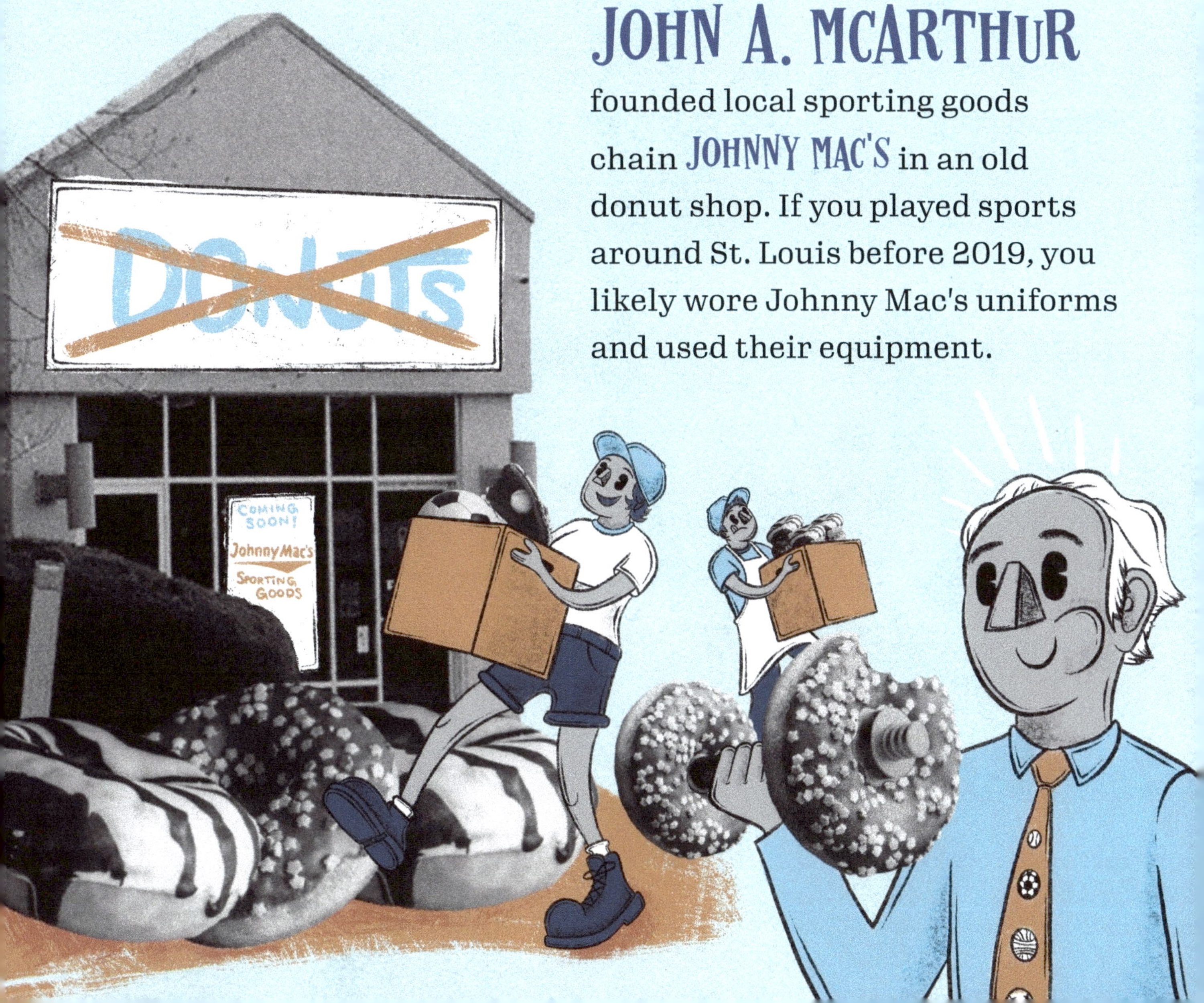

St. Louis is home to the first

MONSTER TRUCK!

The "monster truck" BIGFOOT appeared in public for the first time
in 1979. The first recorded monster truck crash occurred two years
later as the truck crushed two cars in a field outside St. Louis.

WILBUR G. FIENUP

and his father,
William, were the
inventors of the
pop-open biscuit
can, which led
to Pillsbury's
Poppin' Fresh
DoughBoy.

According to local legend,
the Tompkins Riverside restaurant is **HAUNTED.**

A long time ago, Francis Kremer built the house for his family. Supposedly, his mother-in-law's spirit now haunts the house on Main Street in St. Charles. Many customers have spoken of strange events, including glasses, drinks, and utensils **DISAPPEARING** with no explanation and water glasses mysteriously spilling.

GOOEY BUTTER CAKE is a famous St. Louis treat, but did you know it was created by accident?

St. Louis Pastries Bakery worker JOHNNY HOFFMAN accidentally switched the amounts of butter and flour in a recipe, and gooey butter cake was born.

In 1873, **SUSAN BLOW** opened the **FIRST KINDERGARTEN** in the United States in Carondelet. Her first class at Des Peres Elementary School had 42 students. How many students are in your classroom?

JIMMY JOE

was a purebred Clydesdale who pulled just-married couples around Tower Grove Park and sometimes offered his head and snout to be petted. Jimmy Joe gave about **2,700 RIDES** during his lifetime.

St. Louis businessman **BOB HERMANN** started what became the National Professional Soccer League. He belongs to the National Soccer Hall of Fame and the St. Louis Soccer Hall of Fame.

The Hardscrabble cabin at **GRANT'S FARM** was not only owned by a former United States President, but it was also once owned by **CYRUS BLANKE**, the owner of a local coffee and tea business.

This book is dedicated to my son Theodore, who originally gave me the idea for this book, and my daughter Josephine. I hope you both continue to love books as much as I do.

About the Author

My name is Michael Kleckner. I was born and raised in St. Louis County and graduated from the Journalism School at the University of Missouri–Columbia in 2009. I have lived in Kirkwood since 2011 with my wife, Christine; son, Teddy; daughter, Josie; dog, Lucy; and two cats, Truman and Jack.

For all of my adult life, I have been extremely passionate about St. Louis history. I am also an avid reader. I read EVERYTHING. Magazines, newspapers, newsletters, flyers, brochures, etc. This includes everything from West Newsmagazine and the Webster-Kirkwood Times to the Chesterfield Out & About magazine and the Town & Country newsletter. My passion for St. Louis and love for reading combined with my curious nature resulted in the creation of this book.

Thank you to my mother (also an avid reader), Robin Snitzer, for saving me every publication she reads and for buying me nearly every St. Louis history book for birthdays and Christmas. Thank you to my wife for putting up with me and acting like she is interested in my unprompted, unprovoked St. Louis history tours whenever we go anywhere. One day I will give her a date night that doesn't involve me telling her that the restaurant at which we are dining is in a registered historic building.